Believers Foundations Training Manual

OSMOND OWUSU

Library of Congress Control Number: 2016910972
ISBN: Softcover   978-1-5065-1494-9
               eBook   978-1-5065-1537-3

Print information available on the last page.

Rev. date: 24/09/2016

To order additional copies of this book, contact:
Palibrio
1663 Liberty Drive
Suite 200
Bloomington, IN 47403
Toll Free from the U.S.A 877.407.5847
Toll Free from Mexico 01.800.288.2243
Toll Free from Spain 900.866.949
From other International locations +1.812.671.9757
Fax: 01.812.355.1576
orders@palibrio.com
339425

CONTENTS

Chapter 1   Introduction 1

Chapter 2   Assurance of Salvation 4

Chapter 3   The Repentant Life 9

Chapter 4   Christian Perfection 14

Chapter 5   Separation from the World 18

Chapter 6   The Tri-Part Man at Salvation 23

Chapter 7   The Godhead 28

Chapter 8   The Word of God 34

Chapter 9   Prayer and Fasting....................................39

Chapter 10   Christian Life and Growth......................45

Chapter 11   Satanic Kingdom......................................51

Chapter 12   Eternal Judgment 56

Chapter 13   The Resurrection.......................................61

Chapter 14   Baptisms 66

Chapter 15   Christian Ministry 72

Chapter 16   Ministry Offices and Spiritual Gifts........78

Chapter 17   Conclusion 85

CHAPTER 1

INTRODUCTION

The modern church is come a long way with the issues concerning Christian education. In defining Christian education, one may ask what exactly must the body of Christ be taught to know. We are looking at this span from what is taught at bible colleges, seminaries, denominations, local assemblies, home groups, and the foundation of new ministries springing up.

The church is born, sustained, and grows by the Word of God. Therefore it is critical and wise for every church group, which professes the Lord Jesus to be its Head, to examine what is taught more carefully. The enemy can only steal, kill and destroy when the sheep is wallowing in ignorance (**John 10:10**). Biblical ignorance is not to be taken lightly by anyone.

We have a very warped concept of the Word of God. The Holy Scriptures is taken lightly by many. Preachers and teachers pick and choose what will let our congregants feel most comfortable, and not what the Lord would have us hear. To dumb-down congregants, a two-fold formula is used: water it down and make it positive. This makes the Lord's preaching, that of the apostles, Stephen, Philip, and the prophets in the Old Testament look uncouth. The Word of God must remain the Word of God. Take it or leave it. The Lord Jesus warns against adulterating His Word; this includes watering it down to reduce its divine-desired effect. The Word liberates. Teach and preach as the Lord will have you to.

Discipleship goes beyond just a Sunday school class. Some churches have left it entirely to the TV preachers and Facebook preaching. Church leaders have to go back and look at discipleship as the mission mentioned by the Lord Jesus Christ in **Matthew 28:18-20**. On earth, the Lord schooled the early brethren in the Word, and also in prayer. Under the Lord's leading, the early church was immersed in prayer. You cannot divorce active prayer and fasting, coupled with strong biblical instruction from the church. These are essential tools for survival and thriving of the church before the Lord comes for His Bride.

It is therefore expedient and non-negotiable that new believers are immersed in the Word of God and in prayer strongly. As the Lord saves and brings a new believer to join us, what are some of the things which are **basic** non-negotiable doctrines that must be taught? What are some prayer activities we can engage them in to teach prayer in a more practical way?

This manual attempts to capture some of the essentials for the new believer in the Lord Jesus Christ. To get the most out of it, approach it with the mindset that the Lord has something to teach every time. The bible is given to us by the Lord to speak to us. Our expectation is then

(**1 Samuel 3:7, 21**). This manual is designed to let the bible itself do the tutorial. I use the Authorized Version or the KJV.

Each chapter begins with an introduction, followed by some essential questions (about eight questions per chapter). Each question is not directly answered. The new believer is provided with some textual references from the bible. Please you must read **ALL** the text provided for each question, derive meaning from the text and write down your conclusion in the space provided. Although non-exhaustive, I humbly submit that this Manual will provide a good and strong start for the new believer. Reading it as a newsprint without reading the texts will not help.

I will encourage you not to let it end here; keep studying and searching the Holy Scriptures. The bible says that the Word of God is our life (**Deuteronomy 32:46-47**). Study it daily to show yourself approved unto the Lord Jesus Christ (**2 Timothy 2:15**).

CHAPTER 2

ASSURANCE OF SALVATION

Salvation, in the biblical sense, could be defined as to be saved from the power of sin and its eternal consequences. This presupposes that humans after Adam and Eve, have the nature of sin, which must be dealt with. One cannot deny the effects of this sin nature which is all around us from the earliest civilizations to our times. We also feel it as the inner struggle we have when one is swayed to do things contrary to his or her conscience. Our Creator in His infinite mercies and grace has provided both the tools and the process so that we can be victorious in this life and hereafter. Let us read the scriptures and respond to the questions based on the bible (KJV).

- Is every human being born with the sin nature? **Rom 5:12, Gal 3:22, 1 Jn 1:8, Rom 3:23**

_____

_____

_____

_____

_____

_____

_____

- Has God made provisions for salvation that must be accepted and received by a person? **Jn 3:16-18, Rom 1:16, Rom 10:10, Acts 8:27-38, 2 Thessalonians 1:7-10**

_____

_____

_____

_____

_____

_____

- Does God's plan of salvation include human-like beings (clones, human cyborgs, human-animal hybrids, and human-alien hybrids)? **Gen 1:11, 12, 20, 21; Gen 6:1-6, Dan 2:43.**

_____

_____

_____

_____

_____

_____

- Does God's plan of salvation include fallen Satan, angels and demons? **Matt 25:41, Jude 6, Job 38:4-7, John 16:11, Rev 12:12**

_____

_____

_____

_____

_____

_____

_____

- Do we get sinless perfection at salvation? **1 John 1:8, 1 Peter 1:22, Ephesians 5:25-27, Ephesians 4:13, 2 Corinthians 3:18**

_____

_____

_____

_____

_____

_____

_____

- Is God's plan and His tools effective enough to really save? Do we need purgatory? **Hebrews 7:25, Acts 4:12, Romans 1:16, Titus 2:14, Isaiah 49:25, Revelation 20:12-15, Philippians 1:6**

_____

_____

_____

_____

_____

_____

_____

- Are there any emotional or physical bodily feelings when saved? **John 3:16, Acts 2:38-41, Galatians 3:26, Ephesians 2:8, Ephesians 3:12, 17, Romans 10:8-11**

_____

_____

_____

_____

_____

_____

_____

- Does your nature remain the same after salvation? **Hebrews 9:14; Rom 8:10, 13; 1Cor 6:17; 1 Cor 12:13; Eph 2:10; Eph 4:24**

_____

_____

_____

_____

_____

_____

_____

- What are the essential domains by which we sin? **Gen 3:1-6; 1 John 2:15-17; James 4:4**

_____

_____

_____

_____

_____

_____

_____

- Must we have the assurance of being saved? **Titus 1:2; Isaiah 32:17, Heb 6:11; Heb 10:22; Heb 11:6; Heb 10:38; John 14:1-3**

_____

_____

_____

_____

_____

_____

_____

CHAPTER 3

THE REPENTANT LIFE

The Christian life is a life of repentance from the inside out. The dramatic spiritual journey begins when one is born again, and receives a divine remaking which is created in the image of the Lord Jesus Christ. The bible says in **Mark 2:17**, "*When Jesus heard it, he saith unto them, They that are whole have no need of the physician, but they that are sick: I came not to call the righteous, but sinners to repentance.*". False Christianity and the antichrist teaches that you should live however you want, justify your sins because God is love, and that all are sinners, and that no one is perfect, and that you are going through a lot of pain in life, etc. Let us examine what the scriptures is actually teaching us:

- What is repentance? **Hebrews 6:1, Matthew 4:17, Mark 1:15, Proverbs 1:23, Proverbs 28:13**

_____

_____

_____

- What makes a believer repentant, if the born again experience is genuine? **1 John 3:4-10, Psalm 119:11, Romans 5:5, Ephesians 4:30, Colossians 3:10**

_____

_____

_____

_____

_____

_____

- Why do people live in the unrepentant state? **James 3:11-12; 2 Timothy 2:19, Romans 7:17, Titus 3:3, Gal 3:1, Acts 8:9-11**

_____

_____

_____

_____

_____

_____

- Why do believers live the repentant life? **Eph 5:25-27, Matt 5:16, Eph. 2:10; John 15:1-5; 1 Peter 2:9; 1 Peter 1:2; 2 Peter 1:4-8**

_____

_____

_____

_____

_____

_____

_____

- What role is the social environment (media, and the social media) in this journey? **Proverbs 27:17, 1 Corinthians 15:33, Isaiah 25:7, Ephesians 2:2-3**

_____

_____

_____

_____

_____

_____

- Is the repentant life important to the Lord Jesus Christ? Is it God's will? **1 Thess 4:3-4, Rev 3:15-16, Matthew 5:16, Deut 11:8, 12; Deut 32:9, Eph 1:4**

_____

_____

_____

_____

_____

_____

_____

- Are we perpetual sinners even after a genuine salvation experience? **Isaiah 66:2, 1 John 3:1-10, Rev 3:19, Acts 3:19, Matt 4:17, Luke 13:3, 2 Samuel 22:33**

_____

_____

_____

_____

_____

_____

- How would unbelievers react to the repentant believer? **1 John 3:1, 1 Cor 2:14, John 16:33, John 15:19, 2 Tim 3:12, Psalm 119:51, John 3:17-21, 1 John 3:13, Luke 6:22,**

_____

_____

_____

_____

_____

_____

- What lifestyle has the Lord Jesus called Christians into? **Eph 2:1-5, John 15:16, Rom 6:20-23, Eph 2:10, 1 Peter 1:15, 1 Peter 2:9**

_____

_____

_____

_____

_____

_____

_____

CHAPTER 4

CHRISTIAN PERFECTION

One of the household mantras you hear everywhere today is the phrase 'no one is perfect' or you will hear 'I am a work in progress' or 'he who is without sin, cast the first stone' or similar phrases taken completely out of context. Their impact is a very serious affront to the message of the gospel of the Lord Jesus Christ. This is an integral part of the "another gospel" that the Lord warns us about in **2 Corinthian 11:4**, *'For if he that cometh preacheth another Jesus, whom we have not preached, or if ye receive another spirit, which ye have not received, or another gospel, which ye have not accepted, ye might well bear with him'*. Beloved the Lord Jesus warns us again in **Galatians 1:6**,' *I marvel that ye are so soon removed from him that called you into the grace of Christ unto another gospel'*.

It is therefore evident that we have parallel gospels going around posing to be the gospel of the Lord Jesus but are apparent and fake. The authenticity of the Christian life and witness revolves around a walk of holiness and perfection. We shall therefore examine them in the light of the unadulterated Word of God. The paradox is whether the Christian faith implies sinlessness as perfection or there is particular context to this that the Holy Scriptures is teaching us. Let us explore what the Word says.

- Is the Lord Jesus calling believers to live perfect lives? **Gen 6:9, Deut 18:13, Psalm 18:32, 1 Kings 8:61, 1 Kings 15:14, 2 Chron 16:9, Matt 5:48, Lev 20:7, Colossians 1:28; 4:12; 1 Pet 1:15-16, Rev 3:2, 2 Tim 3:17, 1 John 4:17**

_____

_____

_____

_____

_____

_____

_____

- Did the man Christ Jesus learn perfection on earth? **Hebrews 2:10, Hebrews 5:8-9, Philippians 2:1-8,**

_____

_____

_____

_____

_____

_____

- What does biblical perfection mean? **1 Chron 28:9, Luke 9:23, Col 3:3, 5; Matt 19:21, Luke 6:40, John 15:13**

_____

_____

_____

_____

_____

_____

_____

- What is the self-evidence of biblical perfection in a believer's life? **Hebrews 9:14, Acts 24:16, 2 Corinthians 4:2, 1 Timothy 1:19, Colossians 1:10, Isaiah 66:2, 1 John 3:22, Revelation 12:11**

_____

_____

_____

_____

_____

_____

- If the "no one is perfect catch-phrase, is against the gospel, then where is it coming from? **Galatians 3:1, 2 Timothy 3:1-5, 1 Timothy 4:1, Isaiah 14:12, Hosea 4:1-7**

_____

_____

_____

_____

_____

_____

_____

- What type of believers is the Lord looking for? **Genesis 17:1; 2 Chronicles 16:9, John 4:23-24, Eph 5:9, Col 1:10, 1 Thess 2:12**

_____

_____

_____

_____

_____

_____

- What really separates believers from unbelievers? **Matthew 5:13-16, Romans 14:17, Romans 6:13-14, 17-18, Luke 3:8, Matthew 9:13, 2 Sam 22:33, 1 Peter 1:22-23, 2 Cor 7:10, Exodus 19:5, Eph 2:1-5**

_____

_____

_____

_____

_____

_____

CHAPTER 5

SEPARATION FROM THE WORLD

The salvation of a person by the Lord Jesus Christ in the biblical sense, if genuine, will yield a dramatic change in lifestyle, perspectives and worldview. The world system, whose potentate is the devil, is in direct head-on fierce conflict with the Lord Jesus Christ. The scriptures describe and make us aware in **Ephesians 2:2-3**, of who is in charge of this worldly system and what drives it. This demonic system is what characterizes the earthly realm outside the kingdom of the Lord Jesus Christ. When an individual is saved, you must then cut ties with this satanic machinery.

As a new believer in Jesus Christ, you need to be aware of the reality of this system. Through the lens of the Word of God, a look around through the power of His Spirit will alert you of what the Lord Jesus is calling you from. Let's explore the scriptures to discern what the Lord is saying to us concerning the world system.

- Who is in charge of this world system? **Genesis 3:1-7, Rev 12:9, Isaiah 14:12, Ephesians 6:10-13, Luke 4:5-6**

_____

_____

_____

_____

_____

_____

_____

- What drives this satanic world machinery? **Isaiah 14:12-14, Revelation 12:7-9, John 10:10, John 8:44**

_____

_____

_____

_____

_____

_____

- Why is it opposed to the Lord? **Rev 12:7-9, Eph 2:2, John 14:30, John 1:4-5, John 7:7, John 14:17, John 17:16**

_____

_____

_____

_____

_____

_____

- What characterizes this system? **1 John 2:16, Gen 3:4-6, Rom 3:20-28, Eph 2:8-9, Gal 5:24, Eph 2:3, 2 Peter 1:4**

_____

_____

_____

_____

_____

_____

_____

- What is the eternal destiny of this system? **1 John 2:17, John12:31, John 16:11, 1 Corinthians 6:2**

_____

_____

_____

_____

_____

_____

_____

- What should be our attitude to the world system? **2 Cor. 6:14-18, Prov. 8:13, 2 Peter 2:20-22, Mark 9:47, Psalm 97:10**

_____

_____

_____

_____

_____

_____

_____

- What are the implications if someone is overtaken by this system? **James 4:4-5, Mark 8:38, Romans 8, John 15:1-6, Rev 3:14-16**

_____

_____

_____

_____

_____

_____

- Why is separation from the world critical to our walk with Jesus? **1 Cor 11:32, Hebrews 12:8, 1 Cor 15:33, Eph 5:1-11, Matthew 12:30**

_____

_____

_____

_____

_____

_____

- How do we overcome the world system? **1 John 5:4-5, 1 Cor 15:57, 1 Peter 1:3-5, John 17:17, Eph 5:25-26, 1 Tim 4:5, 1 Cor 6:11, 1 John 4:4, Revelation 12:11**

_____

_____

_____

_____

_____

_____

- Does the world embrace true biblical Christian life? **John 16:33, 1 John 3:1, 2 Peter 3:3-9, Matt 4:8, Luke 6:22, 2 Tim 3:12**

_____

_____

_____

_____

_____

_____

CHAPTER 6

THE TRI-PART MAN AT SALVATION

The understanding of our make up as created by the Lord, and taught in the Holy Scriptures, is very critical in understanding the spiritual journey we embark on called the highway of holiness (**Isaiah 35:8-9**). This will open our eyes to see the process of sanctification in a different light. This will also bring to light the foundation for the operation of spiritual gifts. The study will explore the different aspects of our being and how each functions.

Most people discount the spiritual aspects of humanity even from biblical standpoint, opening up a lot of confusion around the question of spiritual gifts. This also throws light on how demon possession, and the practice of witchcraft and new age experience work in people. We will delve into what our make-up is as created by the Lord Jesus. We will look at the human state before salvation, and how each component is affected at salvation.

- Does everyone, who exists by the divinely prescribed way, have distinct parts of being? **Genesis 2:7, 1 Thess 5:23, Hebrews**

4:12, 1 Cor 15:44, Zechariah 12:1, John 3:6, 1 Cor 6:20, Proverbs 20:27

_____

_____

_____

_____

_____

_____

_____

- What is the state of our spirits before salvation? **John 3:3, 1 Corinthians 2:14, Luke 8:10, Matthew 7:6, Job 32:8**

_____

_____

_____

_____

_____

_____

- What is the state of our soul before salvation? **Prov 21:10, 1 Peter 2:11, Hab 2:4, Ezekiel 18:4, Prov 19:16, Luke 19:10, 2 Cor 4:3**

_____

_____

_____

_____

_____

_____

_____

- What is the state of our body before salvation? **1 Corinthians 6:19, Romans 8:11-13, Colossians 3:5**

_____

_____

_____

_____

_____

_____

- What is the state of our spirits after salvation? **Ezek 36:26, 1 Cor 6:17, John 3:3, 1 Cor 2:14, Luke 8:10, Matt 7:6, Eph 3:16, Job 32:8, John 4:24, Psalm 32:2**

_____

_____

_____

_____

_____

_____

- What is the state of our soul after salvation? **Hebrews 9:14, James 1:21, 2 Peter 2:8, 3 John 1:2,**

_____

_____

_____

_____

_____

_____

_____

- What happens to our body after salvation? **1 Corinthians 6:19, Romans 8:10-11, 1 Timothy 4:8**

_____

_____

_____

_____

_____

_____

- How do we build up each part? **1 Peter 2:2, 1 Cor 14:4, 14; 1 Peter 1:22, Romans 12:2, 1 John 2:27**

_____

_____

_____

_____

_____

- What are the implications for our spiritual journey? **John 12:25, Mark 8:36, Mark 9:47, Philippians 3:3, 2 Peter 1:5-10, Ezek 18:27, 1 Cor 9:26-27, Revelation 3:15-16**

_____

_____

_____

_____

_____

_____

_____

CHAPTER 7

THE GODHEAD

The quality of one's Christian walk largely depends on the individual's understanding of who God is. Both internal and outward expression of the fear of the Lord, or what we commonly call worship, depends on the individual's theology.

We have four basic theological views. Broadly put, we have Polytheism (many Gods), Pantheism (all is God and God is in everything), Monotheism (One God), and Atheism (no God). There are different opinions and perspectives regarding who God is, across different cultures and eras of human existence. We shall examine basic theology or the study of God through the scriptures. Please let us look at what the scriptures teach.

- Is there one God, many Gods, or no God at all? **Deuteronomy 6:4, James 2:19, 1 Timothy 2:5, Ephesians 4:6**

_____

_____

_____

_____

_____

- Is God a created figment of our imagination? **Gen 18:1-22, Gen 32:30, Exodus 33:11, 1 Samuel 3:1-10, Acts 26:13-18, Rev 1:9-18**

_____

_____

_____

_____

_____

_____

- Can man evolve to become God or do we have ascended masters? **Isaiah 43:10, 1 Cor 1:29, 1 Peter 1:24, Isaiah 14:12-15, 2 Thess 2:3-4**

_____

_____

_____

_____

_____

_____

- Is God an impersonal force or God is a person who can be personally known? **Proverbs 8:17, Jeremiah 29:13, 2 Corinthians 6:17-18**

_____

_____

_____

_____

_____

_____

- Does God have a personal name? **Exodus 6:3, Exodus 20-21, Leviticus 19:12, Matthew 28:19, Acts 2:36-38**

_____

_____

_____

_____

_____

_____

- Does God appreciate Him being put at same level as created beings or images? **Exodus 12:12, Exodus 20:1-6, Deuteronomy 4:15-19, Deuteronomy 17:2-5, 1 Samuel 5:2-5, Romans 1:17-32**

_____

_____

_____

_____

_____

_____

_____

- Is God, our Creator, a collection of super-advanced alien species? **John 1:1-3, Col 1:16-17, Hebrews 1:2, Rev 1:4-8, Deut 32:39**

_____

_____

_____

_____

_____

_____

- If God can be known, how has God revealed Himself to humanity? **Matt 28:19; Genesis 3:8; 1 Samuel 3:6-7; Romans 1:18-20; Heb 1:1-3**

_____

_____

_____

_____

_____

_____

- Is the Son of God also God? **1 John 5:7, John 1:1-14, Rom 9:5, Psalm 2:11-12, Isaiah 9:6-7, Hebrews 1:8, Rev 1:1-18, Rev 5:6**

- Is the Holy Spirit God? **Job 33:4, 1 John 5:7, Luke 1:35, Acts 5:3-4, Acts 20:28, Genesis 1:1-2**

- Can God become better or evolve? **Jeremiah 10:10, Malachi 3:6, James 1:17, Hebrews 13:8, Exodus 3:14, Deuteronomy 33:27,**

_____
_____
_____

- How does the bible describe the faith of the atheist? **Rom. 1:18-32, 2 Pet 2:1, Jude 4, John 12:40, 2 Cor 4:4, 2 Thess 1:7-10**

_____
_____
_____
_____
_____
_____
_____

CHAPTER 8

THE WORD OF GOD

The bible states emphatically that humans are born again by the Word of God, we develop faith by the Word of God (**1 Peter 1:23**), we grow in Christian maturity by the Word of God (**1 Peter 2:2**), the objective standard for faith and conduct is the Word of God (**2 Timothy 3:16-17**), and the sword of the Spirit is the Word of God (**Ephesians 6:17**). Undoubtedly, the Word of God is of supreme importance in the life of every believer. There is no substitute for the Word of God (**Deuteronomy 32:46-47**). Doctrine is discounted for hysteria and experience in some Christian circles which is very dangerous (**Hosea 4:1-14**). Discounting biblical doctrines is simply dumbing down the church, and opens doors for all kinds of teachings of seducing spirits (**1 Timothy 4:1-3**). Your challenge is to keep yourself from deception and so focus on the Lord Jesus Christ (**Mark 13:5**).

Our understanding and parameters of operation in the kingdom of the Lord is based on the Word of God (**Deuteronomy 5:32**). Protecting oneself against deception in these last days depends on your knowing, understanding and application of the Word of God. Therefore if the old dragon has anything to attack, it is the Word of God. Every church community is molded by what comes out of the pulpit. Believers follow the Word of God (**Rev 19:11-14**). Let's explore what the scriptures say about the Word God.

- Does God have books? **Dan. 7:10, Rev. 20:12, Ex. 24:7, Num. 21:14, Deut. 28:61, Isaiah 34:16, Phil. 4:3, Rev. 3:5, Rev. 13:8, Rev. 10:8-11**

_____

_____

_____

_____

_____

_____

_____

- Isn't the bible concocted by men? What makes it the Word of God? **2 Peter 1:19-21, Psalm 68:11, 2 Timothy 3:15-17, Deuteronomy 29:29**

_____

_____

_____

_____

_____

_____

_____

- Is there a Spirit behind the bible or it's just like any book? **John 1:1-3; 1 John 5:7; 1 Sam. 3:7, 21; Gen. 3:8; Rev. 19:11-16; Heb. 1:1-2**

_____

_____

_____

_____

_____

_____

- Why must we build our live on the Word of God? **Psalm 119:89; 1 Peter 1:23; Matt 7:24-25; Luke 6:48; Psalm 1; Col 2:6-10**

_____

_____

_____

_____

_____

_____

- What is God's view about the Word of God? **Psalm 138:2; Ezekiel 12:25; Jer. 1:12; Psalm 119:106; Isaiah 55:10-11**

_____

_____

_____

_____

_____

_____

- How has God been dealing with Humans? **Gen 3:8; Psalm 107:19-20; Psalm 119:130; Eccles 8:4; 1 Tim. 2:5; Isaiah 9:8**

_____

_____

_____

_____

_____

_____

- What's the role of the Word of God spiritual warfare? **Luke 4:2-13; John 1:1-5; Rev. 19:11-16; Eph. 6:10-17; 2 Cor. 10:4-6**

_____

_____

_____

_____

_____

_____

- Can the bible be trusted in all matters? **Psalm 12:6-7; 2 Samuel 22:31; Matthew 5:17-18; John 10:35**

_____

_____

_____

_____

_____

_____

_____

- What is the Bible's basic layout? **Student Research Assignment**

I.   How many books?

II.   What's the span of years from earliest writing to last writer?

III. How were the books put together to form what we have as the bible (canonization)?

IV. Why couldn't there be conflicts in what the bible teaches?

V.   How should we view extra-biblical books, like apocrypha, Jasher, Enoch, etc.?

VI. What's the basic difference between the testaments?

VII. If there are no errors in what it teaches, then why are there many denominations?

VIII. Are all English translations or versions of the bible trustworthy?

_____

_____

_____

_____

_____

_____

CHAPTER 9

PRAYER AND FASTING

Prayer has been one of the most fascinating and confused spiritual disciplines of the Christian faith. We find in the scriptures that Adam and Eve had a discourse with the Voice of God (**Genesis 3:8**). Also the scriptures record that men began to call upon God around the time when Enoch was born (**Genesis 4:26**). The more one investigates this exercise, it becomes apparent who instigates the confusion as always.

Tapping into the spiritual resources the Lord provides, at the direct invitation of the Lord, is through prayer (**Hebrews 4:16**). Some have taken to the habit of discounting prayer totally on the premise that they have figured out how to work things out, therefore prayer is not needed. Don't allow the enemy to lull you into spiritual slumbering. One of the Lord's expectation of His house is found here (**Isaiah 56:7**). If your church is not in that mode, then you need to repent and set things straight. We are admonished to pray without ceasing (**1 Thess. 5:17**), but unfortunately some claim to be smarter than God Himself (sarcastic). Let's dive into the scriptures.

- What is Christian prayer? **Jer. 33:3, Exodus 33:11, 1 Samuel 3:6-11**

_____

_____

_____

_____

_____

_____

_____

- In whose name must we pray, and why do we pray? **John 14:13-14; John 16:23; Exodus 15:1-13; 1 John 1:9; Prov. 28:13; Psalm 95:2; Psalm 116:17; Psalm 28:2; 1 Timothy 2:1; Daniel 9:3**

_____

_____

_____

_____

_____

_____

- From the references, which particular spiritual discipline did all these heroes practice? **Gen. 18:18-33; Exod. 14:15; Exod. 33:11; 1 Sam. 7:9; 1 Sam 12:23; 1 Sam 15:11; 2 Sam 22:1-18; Neh. 1:4-11; Mark 1:35; Job 42:10; Acts 6:4; Acts 16:25**

_____

_____

_____

_____

_____

_____

_____

- What are the implications if believers don't pray? **Matt. 26:41, 2 Chronicles 7:14, Matt. 17:21, Eph. 6:18-19, Col 4:3, Acts 4:31, Acts 12:5-10, Isaiah 52:1-3**

_____

_____

_____

_____

_____

_____

- Are believers allowed to pray to other beings or channel them? Why? **Deut 18:10-13; Deut 8:19; Jeremiah 13:10; 1 Cor. 10:20**

_____

_____

_____

_____

_____

- What could hinder our prayers? **Psalm 15, Psalm 66:18; Job 35:13; 1 Peter 3:7; James 4:3, Isaiah 58:6-11**

_____

_____

_____

_____

_____

_____

- Do all prayers by anyone get automatically answered by the Lord? **Proverbs 1:24-31, Isaiah 59:1, Rom 10:13, Acts 4:10-12, Isaiah 66:1-2**

_____

_____

_____

_____

_____

_____

- Which spirit inhibits believers from praying? **1 Thess. 2:18; Gal 3:1; Matt. 16:18; Dan 10:1-14; 1 Chron. 21:1, Matt 16:23, Eph. 6:10-13**

_____

_____

_____

_____

_____

_____

_____

- How does the Lord see his house with regards to prayer? **Luke 21:36; 1 Thess. 5:17; Isaiah 56:7; Acts 2:42; Acts 3:1; 1 Tim 2:8; Acts 12:5**

_____

_____

_____

_____

_____

_____

- Is fasting out of place in our day? **Matthew 9:15; Matthew 17:21; 1 Cor. 7:5; Daniel 9:3; Psalm 35:13; Acts 14:23; Matthew 6:16**

_____

_____

_____

_____

_____

_____

- Do we pray aloud or silently? **1 Samuel 1:13, Acts 4:24**

_____

_____

_____

_____

_____

_____

_____

CHAPTER 10

CHRISTIAN LIFE AND GROWTH

This chapter explores the basics of the Christian life. Every person is a creature of God, but not all are children of God. The Lord Jesus teaches the spiritual principle of true born-again children of God bearing particular fruits, and the consequences of not bearing His fruit in **John 15**. This is fascinating teaching from the Lord Jesus concerning the concept and reality of Christian fruit-bearing. Everything that has life must grow. We will briefly explore the corrective action of the Lord if a believer falls back.

Some confuse Christian growth to be how one displays spiritual disciplines, and even sometimes some go to the extreme to engage in non-biblical esoteric practices. Examples of these are new age practices, secret societies, contemplative prayer and centering, and other spiritually unclean and contaminating dark practices. Some even confuse being biblical as one's stance against what the scriptures condemn only. We must not forget to promote what the Lord is seeking. Let's explore.

- Is every person a child of God? **John 1:10-13; 2 Timothy 2:19; 1 John 3:5-10; Romans 8:18-22; Gal 3:26; Ephesians 1:12-13**

  _____

  _____

  _____

  _____

  _____

  _____

  _____

- What is the Christian life? **John 15:1-27; Tit. 2:11-15; Rom. 8:1-11; Galatians 5:16; Ephesians 2:10; 1 Peter 2:9; 1 Cor. 6:20**

  _____

  _____

  _____

  _____

  _____

  _____

- Is spiritual growth expected in the Christian life? **Matthew 3:8, John 15:16, John 15:1-8, 2 Peter 3:18, 1 Peter 2:2**

  _____

  _____

_____

_____

_____

_____

_____

- What shows a Christian is growing spiritually? **2 Peter 1:1-14, Galatians 5:22-26, 1 Peter 1:22, Ephesians 4:11-16**

_____

_____

_____

_____

_____

_____

- Are spiritual functions, disciplines or gifts a measure of maturity? **1 Corinthians 3:1-4, 1 Peter 1:22, Leviticus 10:1-3, Matthew 7:22-23**

_____

_____

_____

_____

_____

_____

- What is biblical literacy? **Acts 17:10-11; Ezra 7:10; 1 Samuel 3:7; Hebrews 4:2; John 7:17; James 1:21; 2 Tim. 3:15; Eph. 5:25-27**

- What becomes of a life wholly given to the Lord? **Col 1:10; 2 Peter 1:8; 2 Tim. 2:21; 2 Cor. 9:8; Heb. 13:21; 2 Pet 1:4-9; Matt 25:21**

- Is the Christian life just a matter of the heart? **Ephesians 4:1; Matthew 5:15-16; James 2:17-22; Luke 6:45; 2 Cor. 5:17**

_____

_____

_____

_____

_____

- What could stunt Christian growth? **1 Peter 2:2; John 15:1-8; Romans 8:1-4; Psalm 25:9-14; Psalm 1; Prov. 16:3; Psalm 15, 1 Peter 3:12; 1 John 1:3, 7; Hebrews 10:25**

_____

_____

_____

_____

_____

_____

- How do we avoid deception today? **Mark 13:5; Acts 17:10-11; 1 Peter 5:8; John 17:17; Isaiah 40:28-31; 2 Tim 3:15, Eph 1:17**

_____

_____

_____

_____

_____

_____

- Is Christian fellowship necessary in our walk with God? **Acts 2:42; Jeremiah 3:15; Ephesians 4:11-16; 1 John 5:1; Hebrews 10:25; Deuteronomy 32:30; Joel 1:14; John 17:22**

_____

_____

_____

_____

_____

_____

_____

CHAPTER 11

SATANIC KINGDOM

The idea of the existence of Satan or devil can be seen in many cultures but in different contexts. In the scriptures, the Lord Jesus spoke more about the devil and hell than any other preacher. Today our culture has so much silenced the truth to the extent that preachers do not talk about Satan or hell. What does the Lord mean in **Jeremiah 51:20?** We hear about spiritual warfare, but what exactly is the Christian in conflict with? Can ignorance or unbelief in spiritual matters exonerate and excuse us from this conflict?

One cannot understand what is going on in the world around us until you discover what the scriptures reveal about Satan and his minions. Some preachers read **Ephesians 6:12** very awkwardly and get their churches to have this warped view of the spiritual reality that the bible demonstrates over and over to exist and is active. They read **Ephesians 6:12** as **"For we wrestle not…."**. They just end there, deliberately living their lives and preaching as if the adversary of humanity does not exist. They just pride themselves in scriptural ignorance, and thereby plunging their adherents into same. Let's take a plunge into the unadulterated eternal Word of God.

- Is Satan a myth or a particular spirit person? **Rev 12:9; John 8:44; Isaiah 14:12; 1 Peter 5:8; 1 Thess. 2:18; Rev 12:10-12**

_____

_____

_____

_____

_____

_____

_____

- Where has been his location? **Ezekiel 28:14, 16; Luke 10:18; Job 1:6-12; Ephesians 2:2; Revelation 20:10**

_____

_____

_____

_____

_____

_____

- Does Satan have a functional kingdom? **Luke 4:5-7, Colossians 1:13, 2 Corinthians 4:4, Ephesians 6:10-13, Luke 11:18**

_____

_____

_____

_____

_____

_____

_____

- How does he operate against the church? **Isaiah 14:12-14; 2 Cor. 11:13; Jude 4; Gal 3:1; Acts 8:9-10; Luke 8:4-15; Acts 20:26-32**

_____

_____

_____

_____

_____

_____

_____

- What are some of his agents who work with him? **Matt 12:30; Eph 6:10-12; Jude 1:3-4; Psalm 2:1-4, Acts 13:6-8, Ezek 13:18-23, Exodus 22:18**

_____

_____

_____

_____

_____

_____

- What is Satan's main opposition in the human realm? **1 John 5:19; Matthew 16:18; Luke 10:19; Rev 12:11; Eph. 1:18-23**

_____

_____

_____

_____

_____

_____

- Who are the Prisoners of War in this warfare? **Colossians 1:13, Revelation 13:8, Hebrews 3:12, 2 Timothy 2:19, Romans 6:13-18**

_____

_____

_____

_____

_____

_____

- How do believers prevail in this battle? **Mark 9:29; Eccles. 10:8; Col. 3:1-3; Rom 13:14; Eph. 6:10-18; Rev. 12:11; 1 Thess. 5:17**

_____

_____

_____

_____

_____

_____

_____

- What are in our arsenal? **2 Cor. 10:4; Eph 6:10-18; Deut. 11:8; Rev. 12:11; Rev. 8:3-5; 1 John 5:4; Hebrews 4:16; Psalm 9:2-3, Isaiah 9:5**

_____

_____

_____

_____

_____

_____

- How do we use our weaponry? **James 4:6; Psalm 25:12; Joshua 5:13-15, Romans 8:14, Matt 11:12, 1 Tim 1:8, Ephesians 6:10-18**

_____

_____

_____

_____

_____

_____

CHAPTER 12

ETERNAL JUDGMENT

The biblical truth of judgment is very intrinsically woven and intertwined into the very fabric of eternal truth. There are some philosophical ideas floating around the idea. All doctrines of the Christian faith come directly from the Edenic account of human history. The salvation plan of God, the Jewish history and worship system, the incarnation of Jesus Christ, the divine blueprint of putting back his creation into order and making of the enemies of Christ His footstool are all of being because of judgment. The spiritual fact and reality of sin, convoluted with the justice nature of God implies judgment must be declared and enforced (**Genesis 3:7-19**).

The good news of the gospel is because of the consequences of sin, judgment and hell fire (**John 16:8, John 5:22**). The love of God is demonstrated to save us from such. We need to understand that the truth of eternal judgment make the idea of universal salvation of humankind nonsense, which says that all humans will be saved in the end (**2 Thess. 1:7-9**). A second movement is the satanic one world religion. This claims that all religions lead to God (**John 14:6**). The guise that God is love alone is a big insult to Jehovah; indirectly asserting that He is not just and righteous. Please join me as we take the exciting journey through the scriptures.

- What is this "judge not" thing? **Luke 6:37; John 7:24; 1 Cor. 2:12-16; Matthew 7:4-5; Ephesians 5:11; 1 Cor. 10:12**

_____

_____

_____

_____

_____

_____

- Is affirming a conditional predictive prophecy in the Word of God judging? **Colossians 1:28; Acts 20:27; 1 Timothy 5:1, 20; Titus 1:13; 2 Timothy 4:2; Titus 2:5**

_____

_____

_____

_____

_____

_____

- Why is Universalism of the anti-Christ spirit? **John 14:6; John 10:7-14; 2 Thess. 1:8; 1 Peter 4:7; John 3:16-21; Jude 1:5-7; Matt 18:9; Luke 15:10**

_____

_____

_____

_____

_____

_____

_____

- Why is ecumenism dangerous to the Christian faith? **Matt. 25:32-46; Rev. 18:4; Rev. 13:8-15; Rom. 1:17-32; Deut. 4:16-19; Eph. 5:11**

_____

_____

_____

_____

_____

_____

- What is the eternal destiny of the wicked? **Jude 1:7; 2 Thess 1:6-9; Revelations 20:10-15; Revelation 21:8; Revelation 22:10-16**

_____

_____

_____

_____

_____

_____

_____

- What is the eternal judgement and destiny of the believer? **Rom. 14:10; 2 Cor. 5:10; 1 Cor. 3:11-17; John 14:1-3; 1Thess. 4:14-18; Matt.25:14-21**

_____

_____

_____

_____

_____

_____

- What's the believer's role in the judgment of the world and angels? **Psalm 96:12-13, John 5:22, Jude 1:14-15, 1 Corinthians 6:2-3**

_____

_____

_____

_____

_____

_____

- Could people escape the eternal judgment with technology? **Isaiah 2:12-22; Revelations 6:12-17; Psalms 2:1-3**

CHAPTER 13

THE RESURRECTION

The resurrection is the cornerstone of the Christian faith. The Lord Jesus made a very profound and provocative statement in **John 11:25**, *"Jesus said unto her, I am the resurrection, and the life: he that believeth in me, though he were dead, yet shall he live."* But what exactly is the resurrection? Is it the same as someone been raised from the dead? Paul was very passionate about knowing the Lord Jesus in a more continual powerful transformation which he mentions is through the power of the resurrection. Paul was yearning for the fullness of the power of God which makes the resurrection possible, and how we experience snippets of it in our lifetime (**Philippians 3:10**).

We have to understand this all important phenomena which the Lord wrought for all saints to experience. Let's jump right into the scriptures from the unadulterated Word of God.

- Is reincarnation biblical? **Heb. 9:27; John 5:28-29; Luke 16:19-31**

- Why did the Lord institute the resurrection? **John 5:21-29; Matthew 22:31-33; Job 19:25-27**

- What does the resurrection prove? **Acts 4:33, Romans 1:3-4, 1 Corinthians 15:12-22**

_____
_____
_____
_____

- What current derivatives do believers get from the resurrection? **Romans 6:1-14, Ephesians 1:15-23, Colossians 3:1-7**

_____
_____
_____
_____
_____
_____

- What assurance do we derive from the resurrection? **Acts 17:31; Ephesians 1:15-23; John 5:25-29; 1 Cor. 15:51-58; 1 Thess. 4:16; Rom 8:11; 2 Tim. 2:8-13**

_____
_____
_____
_____
_____
_____

- Which spiritual power makes the resurrection possible? **Romans 8:11, Romans 1:4, Romans 6:4**

_____

_____

_____

_____

_____

_____

- What were the bodily properties of the Lord Jesus after His resurrection? **John 20:19, 26; Luke 24:30-43; Romans 6:9**

_____

_____

_____

_____

_____

_____

- Would believers receive the same body type as the Lord Jesus at the resurrection? **1 Cor. 15:50; 1 John 3:2; 1 Cor. 15:42-45**

_____

_____

_____

_____

_____

_____

- What hope do we have in the future biblical fact of the resurrection? **1 Peter 1:3; Hebrews 11:35; 1 Corinthians 15:12-13, 21, 42; Acts 24:15**

_____

_____

_____

_____

_____

_____

_____

- Would unbelievers experience the resurrection? **Acts 24:15, John 5:24-30, Daniel 12:2**

_____

_____

_____

_____

_____

_____

Chapter 14

Baptisms

Baptism in water is one of the ordinances commanded by the Lord Jesus to be observed by His church. The other ordinance is the Lord's Supper. There are some churches and ministers of the gospel who are puffed up enough to discount these two ordinances; professing themselves to be more wise and spiritual than the command Giver Himself. Believers and church groups must humble ourselves and follow what the word of God is teaching us. We may not understand everything to the fullness but we surely will in due course. Our job is to obey the Lord; period. To obey is always better than sacrifice and convenience.

Baptism simply means to immerse. This is borrowed from the Greek word "baptizo". The concept is that the individual is completely immersed in a spiritual phenomenon literally or symbolically. This concept shreds completely systems where people are supposedly "baptized" by simply sprinkling stuff on them. This doesn't depict the spiritual meaning, and is therefore a deviation from biblical truth. Let's explore together.

- What are the basic types of baptisms that we have? **Matthew 28:18-20; Acts 19:1-6; Matthew 3:11; Luke 3:16; John 1:33**

_____

_____

_____

_____

_____

_____

- Why do we baptize people in water? **Matthew 28:19; Romans 6:3-5; Acts 2:41.**

_____

_____

_____

_____

_____

- Who qualifies for water baptism, and who does the baptizing? **Acts 8:35-38; Acts 19:3-5; Acts 2:38; Matthew 3:11; Matthew 28:19-21**

_____

_____

_____

_____

_____

_____

_____

- Does water baptism save? **Ephesians 2:5-9; Romans 10:9-13**

_____

_____

_____

_____

_____

- What makes a water baptism authentic? **Acts 2:38; Romans 10:9-13; Acts 8:37-38; Mark 16:15-16**

_____

_____

_____

_____

_____

_____

- Is baptism with the Holy Spirit legitimate today? **Matt 3:11; Acts 2:1-4; Joel 2:28-29; Acts 2:15-18, 33, 38-39**

_____

_____

_____

_____

_____

_____

_____

- Who qualifies for Holy Spirit baptism, and who does the baptizing? **Acts 2:39; John 3:3-5; Luke 11:9-13; Matt 3:11; Joel 2:28; Luke 24:49**

_____

_____

_____

_____

_____

_____

- Why does the Lord Jesus baptize believers with the Holy Spirit? **Acts 1:8; Luke 24:49; 1 Corinthians 4:20; Matthew 11:12; Acts 8:9-13**

_____

_____

_____

_____

_____

_____

- What makes Holy Spirit baptism authentic? **Luke 11:9-13; Matt. 3:11; James 4:3; 1 Timothy 5:22; Acts 8:18; 1 Timothy 4:14**

_____

_____

_____

_____

_____

_____

- What is the initial evidence of baptism of the Holy Spirit? **Acts 2:1-4; Acts 10:34-38; Acts 19:3-6**

_____

_____

_____

_____

_____

_____

- Does every believer have to be baptized with the Holy Spirit? **Acts 1:8; 1 Corinthians 4:20; Job 13:8; Luke 24:47-49**

_____

_____

_____

_____

_____

_____

- Did people hear other earthly languages when tongues was spoken besides Acts 2? **Acts 2:1-4; Acts 10:34-38; Acts 19:3-6**

_____

_____

_____

_____

_____

_____

_____

CHAPTER 15

CHRISTIAN MINISTRY

Ministry simply means serving. Therefore direct Christian ministry implies, fulfilling your part of the assignment of Christ using His resources and in His way. Indirect Christian ministry will be supporting the cause of Christ by how we live and work which are not directly related to the propagation of the gospel. This means that all Christian ministries must be purposed to fulfill the earthly ministry of Christ (**Isaiah 61:1-9**), which is summarized beautifully in **Matthew 28:18-20**, and also **Ephesians 4:11-18**.

The Lord Jesus does not force anyone to serve Him. Notwithstanding, the question that everyone has to contend with is **Luke 11:23**. If the love we have for Him grows cold, then we lose our drive to win souls, serve, disciple others, or do anything to promote the cause of Christ. We then get more selfish and self-centered. We don't want our love for the Lord to grow cold (**Matthew 24:12**), but rather we want to be **Romans 12:11**. If you are a servant of the Lord, He is saying occupy till He comes (**Luke 19:13**). Let's explore more.

- Why does the Lord expect every believer to be involved in ministry? **1 Peter 2:9; Rev 1:6; 1 Thess. 1:9; Hebrews 9:14; Eph. 4:11-16**

_____

_____

_____

_____

_____

_____

_____

- Are believers spiritually qualified to be part of the ministry generally? **1 Peter 2:9; Ephesians 2:30; Acts 2:33, 38-39; John 1:11-13; John 3:1-5**

_____

_____

_____

_____

_____

_____

- Is any training necessary? **Ephesians 4:11-16; 2 Timothy 2:2**

_____

_____

_____

_____

_____

_____

_____

- Would there be more spiritual qualifications for specific functions? **Rom 6:22; Eph. 4:11; Acts 13:2; Exod. 30:26-30; Ezra 7:10; Micah 3:8; 2 Tim 2:15; Heb. 13:17; 2 Corinthians 3:6**

_____

_____

_____

_____

_____

_____

- What should be the focus of our ministry? **2 Cor. 4:5; Col 3:17; John 8:29; Matthew 6:33; 1 Peter 4:11; 1 Cor. 7:20; 1 Cor. 4:2; Col 1:7**

_____

_____

_____

_____

_____

_____

- What should be our source in ministering? **Acts 1:8; 2 Cor. 9:8; Micah 3:8; Gen 22:8; Rom 8:14; 1 Samuel 17:47; 2 Tim 4:17**

_____

_____

_____

_____

_____

_____

_____

- What aspects of our lives matter in ministry? **Matthew 28:20; Rom 8:32; Psalm 91:9-16; Matthew 7:11; John 16:23-24**

_____

_____

_____

_____

_____

_____

- Is it wise to seek or take personal glory when ministering? **1 Cor. 10:31; 1 Peter 4:11; Isaiah 42:8; 1 Cor. 6:20; 1 Peter 4:16**

_____

_____

_____

_____

_____

_____

- Is there any opposition to Christian ministry? **Matt 11:12, Eph. 6:10-12; Dan 10; Acts 13:8; 2 Tim 3:8; 2 Tim 4:15, 1 Thess 2:18**

_____

_____

_____

_____

_____

_____

_____

- Do we need mentoring in ministry? **Matt 11:29; 1 Cor. 11:1; 1 Cor. 4:16; Exodus 24:13, 2 Kings 2, 1 Tim 1:2, Titus 1:4**

_____

_____

_____

_____

_____

_____

- Are there divine rewards in ministry? **Matthew 25:15-23; Hebrews 6:10; Isaiah 54:17; Psalm 34:22**

_____

_____

_____

_____

_____

_____

_____

CHAPTER 16

MINISTRY OFFICES AND SPIRITUAL GIFTS

Positionally, the church is the most potent spiritual force on the planet (**Matthew 16:18**). The arch-enemy is able to plague the church so much so that we are, apparently, imploding on doctrines and minor issues. The effectual system and resources the Lord has bestowed on the church is totally ignored, and we are wallowing in our own stuff as the world is plunged headlong into moral chaos and darkness.

On this topic, we have the extreme cessationists; who cannot provide even ONE scriptural text to back their claim. Despite the fact that the Lord devoted three whole chapters to teach about them, arrogance is powerful enough to block the truth from such brethren. We also have those who claim to be biblical but yet in denial; mostly because of fakery in showmanship and human experience. We also have those claim to believe but yet operate in excesses. We also have the bunch who simply ridicule and insult the Lord on this; even in the face of the teaching of the scriptures as we are about to see. Some even claim we don't need any of the gifts today. Some also have the fear of the unknown; making them abhor the grace of God in ministry altogether.

With all humility, I want to submit that the church is operating below capacity, and hell is swallowing up sinners in record numbers. The church is unable to effectively deal with new converts who may have some experience in the occult and witchcraft. Local churches cower in the face of a total onslaught satanic attacks through local covens. The Lord has provided all that we need.

Some even claim that these gifts are a thing of the past because of **1 Corinthians 13:8**," *Charity never faileth: but whether there be prophecies, they shall fail; whether there be tongues, they shall cease; whether there be knowledge, it shall vanish away.*" I submit to you that in whichever context you want to look at this verse, you also must conclude and contend that knowledge has ceased today as well.

Let us explore from the Holy Scriptures (**1 Corinthians 12:1**).

- What are the categories of the callings and gifts? **1 Cor. 12:1-6**

_____

_____

_____

_____

_____

_____

- Categorize all the gifts based on the three categories above **1 Cor. 12:7-11, Ephesians 4:8-12, 1 Cor. 12:27-28, Romans 12:3-8**

_____

_____

_____

_____

_____

_____

_____

- Are spiritual gifts scripturally legitimate today? **Joel 2:28-29; Matthew 3:11; Luke 24:49; Acts 1:8; Acts 2:1-4; Acts 2:33; Acts 10:46; Acts 19:6; 1 Cor. 1:5-8; 1 Cor. 12-14; 1 Tim 1:6**

_____

_____

_____

_____

_____

_____

- Does scripture encourage us into these gifts OR away from them? **1 Cor. 1:7; 1 Cor. 12:7, 31; 1 Cor. 14:1, 5,26,31,39; Num. 11:29, 1 Tim. 4:14, 2 Tim. 1:6**

_____

_____

_____

_____

_____

_____

_____

- What does "being Biblical" in the context of spiritual gifts mean? **Deuteronomy 29:29; Acts 4:19; 1 Corinthians 14:37; Ezra 7:10**

_____

_____

_____

_____

_____

_____

- How are we to operate these gifts and callings? **1 Cor. 12:28-13:13; 1 Cor. 4:6; 1 Peter 5:5; Psalm 145:15; Isaiah 40:31; Jer. 14:22, Galatians 5:22-23; 2 Peter 1:3-12**

_____

_____

_____

_____

_____

_____

- Why is the baptism done by the Lord Jesus Christ under such intense attack? **Matt. 3:11, Isaiah 14:12-14, Eph. 6:10-12, 2 Cor. 2:11, Eph. 1:15-19, Ps 119:130**

_____

_____

_____

_____

_____

_____

_____

- How many types of tongues could there be? **Acts 2:1-13; Acts 10:42-48; Acts 19:1-8; 1 Cor. 13:1; 1 Cor. 14:2; 13-19**

_____

_____

_____

_____

_____

_____

- Could you broadly categorize the Gifts of the Holy Spirit into 3? **1 Corinthians 12:7-11**

_____

_____

_____

_____

_____

_____

- Why are these gifts of the Holy Spirit not something we learn? **1 Cor. 12:7; Acts 2:1-4; Matthew 3:11; Acts 2:33; 1 Samuel 10:10-12**

_____

_____

_____

_____

_____

_____

_____

- Does the bible assume manifestations of Holy Spirit gifts to be normal church experience? **James 5:13-18; 1 Cor. 14:26-31; Acts 13:1-3**

_____

_____

_____

_____

_____

_____

_____

- Does the Holy Spirit cause a believer to lose self-control with a manifestation, or can the believer control himself/herself? **2 Timothy 1:7; 1 Corinthians 14:3; Ephesians 5:18**

_____

_____

_____

_____

_____

_____

_____

- Which gift or ministry office could the church afford to lose today? **Eph. 4:11-16; 1 Cor. 12:28. 1 Cor. 14:1; 1 Thess. 5:20, Luke 24:49, Acts 1:8, Acts 11:26-28**

_____

_____

_____

_____

_____

_____

_____

CHAPTER 17

CONCLUSION

In this age of deliberate dumbing down of the body of Christ (**Amos 8:10, 2 Timothy 3:1-5, Matthew 22:29**), living the life of a "Berean" is very vital and indispensable for personal survival (**Acts 17:10-11, Colossians 3:16**). It is necessary and expedient to allow the Word of God to shine forth in one's life to be fruitful in every area of one's life (**Psalm 1**).

The Word of God is the power of God. To achieve victory on this planet, one must follow the Word of God (**Revelations 19:11-13**). The divine true Light, which lighteth every man that cometh into the world (**John 1:9**). The darkness in this life cannot comprehend the Light, neither can the darkness overcome the Light. Totally embrace and receive the engrafted Word of the Lord God Almighty to walk in total victory.

The time to walk and live in biblical ignorance must be over for you and your family (**Psalm 119:130**). The battle is real. Don't allow yourself to be ignorant of the devices of the adversary Satan (**2 Corinthians**

2:11). The armor of the believer as outlined in **Ephesians 6:12-17**, is a graphic display of the effectual utilization of the Word of God in the life of the believer against the fierce forces of evil.

Never let anyone deceive you that prayer is a waste of time. We must be strong in the Lord and in the power of His might (**Ephesians 6:10**). Prayerfulness in all manner of prayer is stated clearly as the essence of the life of victory of the believer. You don't want to be a powerless believer by denying prayer in your life (**Ephesians 6:18**). Therefore those who deny the divine power available to the believer must be shunned (**2 Timothy 3:5**).

May the Lord Jesus Christ, the only potentate bless you in all areas of your life. May your head never lack the oil of the Lord Jesus (**Psalm 92:10**), may you be like the tree planted by the rivers of water; so shall you bear your fruit in the right timing and seasons determined by the Lord Jesus Christ (**Psalm 1**). May every satanic assignment against you and your family be frustrated and destroyed. And the very God of peace sanctify you wholly; and I pray God your whole spirit and soul and body be preserved blameless unto the coming of our Lord Jesus Christ (**2 Thessalonians 5:23**). I speak life and blessings to you.

Printed in the United States
By Bookmasters